MW01107336

# WEIRD
# ROBOTS

WORLD
BOOK

www.worldbook.com

World Book, Inc.
180 North LaSalle Street
Suite 900
Chicago, Illinois 60601
USA

For information about other "Robots" titles, as well as other World Book print and digital publications, please go to www.worldbook.com or call 1-800-WORLDBK (967-5325).

For information about sales to schools and libraries, call 1-800-975-3250 (United States) or 1-800-837-5365 (Canada).

Library of Congress Cataloging-in-Publication Data for this volume has been applied for.

Robots
ISBN: 978-0-7166-4128-5 (set, hc.)

Weird Robots
ISBN: 978-0-7166-4138-4 (hc.)

Also available as:
ISBN: 978-0-7166-4148-3 (e-book)

Printed in China by RR Donnelley,
Guangdong Province
1st printing May 2019

## Staff

*Writer:* Jeff De La Rosa

**Executive Committee**

*President*
Geoff Broderick

*Vice President, Finance*
Donald D. Keller

*Vice President, Marketing*
Jean Lin

*Vice President, International*
Maksim Rutenberg

*Vice President, Technology*
Jason Dole

*Director, Human Resources*
Bev Ecker

**Editorial**

*Director, New Print*
Tom Evans

*Managing Editor*
Jeff De La Rosa

*Editor*
William D. Adams

*Librarian*
S. Thomas Richardson

*Manager, Contracts
and Compliance
(Rights and Permissions)*
Loranne K. Shields

*Manager, Indexing Services*
David Pofelski

**Digital**

*Director, Digital Product
Development*
Erika Meller

*Digital Product Manager*
Jon Wills

**Graphics and Design**

*Senior Art Director*
Tom Evans

*Senior Visual
Communications Designer*
Melanie Bender

*Media Editor*
Rosalia Bledsoe

**Manufacturing/
Production**

*Manufacturing Manager*
Anne Fritzinger

*Production Specialist*
Curley Hunter

*Proofreader*
Nathalie Strassheim

# Contents

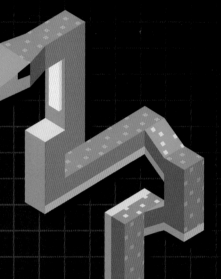

Terms defined in the glossary are in type **that looks like this** on their first appearance on any spread (two facing pages).

# introduction

Imagine a robot. If you are like most people, you probably picture something that looks a bit like a mechanical person. Your robot might have arms with some kind of "hands" or **grippers.** It may have a hard "skin" of metal or plastic. The robot may roll along on wheels or even walk on humanlike legs. Does it have eyes that glow? Does it speak with a mechanical voice?

Some real-life robots fit this traditional idea of what a robot should look like—but certainly not all of them. After all, a robot's design is limited only by its inventor's imagination. And robot inventors come up with some pretty wild ideas.

In this book, you will meet some of those *other* robots. Some crawl like bugs or slither like snakes. Others have soft bodies or are too small to be seen without a microscope. Some can even change their shape or make more of their own kind. So forget what you think you know about robots. Things are about to get a little weird.

**Thinking outside the box**
Inventors have often imagined a robot as something like a mechanical person. But modern robot makers are experimenting with all kinds of forms. The robots shown here have more in common with a snake (left), an octopus (top), and a gecko (right) than the traditional humanoid model.

# The Robot Zoo

Robot inventors have always looked to living things for inspiration. Many robots are **humanoid,** for example. Humanoid robots are designed to look and move like human beings. The humanoid form has many advantages. An advanced humanoid robot should be able to do many things that people do. It could work in our homes and offices without ramps or other special accommodations. It could use tools and devices designed for human hands.

The humanoid form also has limitations. These limitations have led inventors to pattern robots after other animals.

One limitation of the humanoid form is that it can be difficult to balance on two legs. The robot RoboSimian solves this problem by being able to move in a more apelike way. RoboSimian rolls around on four wheels. But when the going gets tough, RoboSimian walks on all fours—much the same way an ape does.

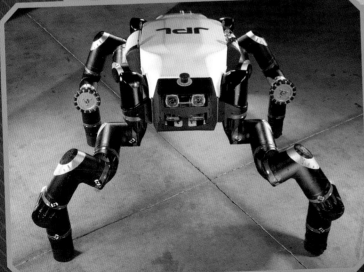

**Spider monkey**
The robot RoboSimian was developed to respond to disasters, climbing over rubble and using stairs, ladders, and tools. *Simian* means *ape* or *monkey*.

# Bionic Kangaroo

Apes are far from the only animals to have inspired robot versions. The German company Festo demonstrated a **prototype** of a robot called the Bionic Kangaroo in 2014. The robot hops from place to place much as does a living kangaroo or wallaby.

The Bionic Kangaroo can balance on two legs. It can hop 2 ½ feet (0.8 meters). The hops are powered in part by springs in the robot's legs. The legs also have "muscles" driven by bursts of compressed air.

**Boing-boing 'bot**
The Bionic Kangaroo hops just like its living counterpart. The robot's inventors added arms and a tail for balance— and a head, just for show.

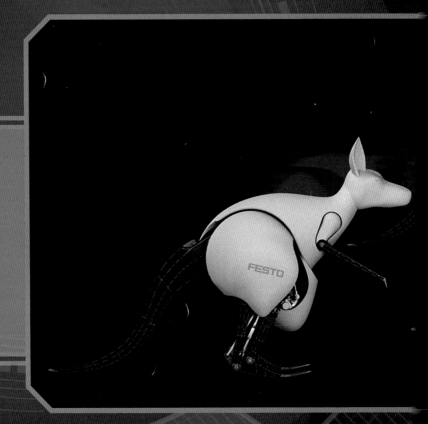

Living kangaroos make use of a special strategy to save energy. As a kangaroo lands, special tendons in its legs stretch out. The tendons act like springs, storing energy for the next jump. This strategy helps the kangaroo to hop over and over without getting tired. The Bionic Kangaroo's mechanical springs work in much the same way.

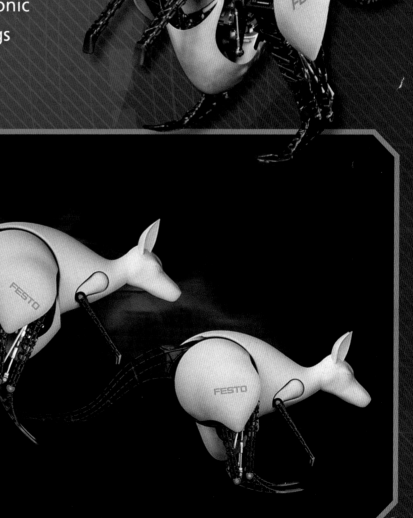

# Bug-inspired

Insects are some of nature's most incredible movers and shakers. Think of all the places ants, bees, and beetles can crawl, fly, and climb. Many insects can lift several times their body weight and perform other amazing feats. And insects do it all with a relatively simple brain and nervous system. It is no wonder that robot designers have looked to insects for inspiration.

One common type of insectlike robot is called a **hexapod.** *Hexapod* comes from Greek words meaning *six feet.* Hexapod robots have six legs, just like insects. The robot can move one or more legs and still keep several feet on the ground. This ability makes hexapod robots very stable.

Extra legs come in handy when crossing rough ground. LAURON is an experimental hexapod built by engineers at the Research Center for Information Technology in Karlsruhe, Germany. LAURON's movement is patterned after that of a stick insect, or walking stick. The robot can map out its surroundings, picking a path across ground rough enough to stop other robots in their tracks.

**LAURON** is a robot designed for scientific exploration and rescue missions. It can use its six legs to creep in where other robots fear to tread. LAURON's green body also glows in the dark!

HELLO, MY NAME IS:

# Genghis

One of the weirdest robots ever built was the **hexapod** robot Genghis *(JEHNG gihs).* This six-legged stalker followed people around by detecting their body heat. Genghis did not use sophisticated computer smarts to creep on its prey. In fact, Genghis had no complex central control system at all. Instead, Genghis's various motors, **sensors,** and **microprocessors** were connected to one another in a network. Each part followed its own simple set of instructions, acting and reacting to the parts around it. The parts worked independently, but together they produced behavior that appeared complex and purposeful.

## AUTONOMY

**HIGH**

Genghis could stalk its prey without human assistance or even complex programming.

## CRAZY LEGS

Each of Genghis's legs could detect its own position and react to the positions of the other legs.

## WHISKERS

Genghis could detect and avoid obstacles in its path using a pair of robot "whiskers."

## SIZE

Genghis was about as big as a house cat.

## MAKER

Genghis was the brainchild of the famous Australian inventor Rodney Brooks. Brooks built the robot in 1989 while working at the Massachusetts Institute of Technology (MIT).

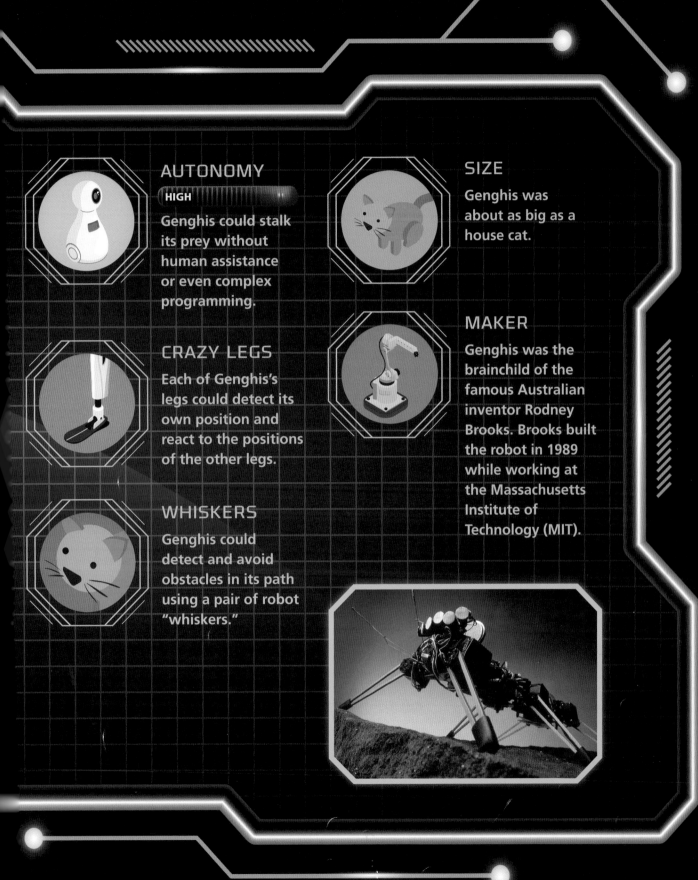

# Birds and Bees

Inventors have already filled the skies with robotic aircraft, sometimes called unmanned aerial vehicles or **drones.** Traditional drones are simply smaller, remote-controlled versions of airplanes or helicopters. But inventors are working to develop drones—and eventually **autonomous** robots— that look and fly more like animals.

In 2011, the American technology company AeroVironment, Inc. unveiled its Nano Hummingbird. This palm-sized drone looks and flies like a hummingbird. Hummingbirds flap their

## The early bird
Nano Hummingbird was the first fully operational, life-sized hummingbird-like drone. This early bird got the worm—a big government contract for its manufacturer.

wings dozens of times per second, allowing them to fly in any direction and even hover in place. The Nano Hummingbird was designed as an experimental spy drone. It has a camera and can fly in and out of buildings.

On the tiny end of things, inventors at Harvard University have developed an insect-inspired robot called the RoboBee. This 1-inch (3-centimeter) robot resembles a tiny flying insect. The first RoboBee models needed to be connected by wire to power and control systems. But engineers hope to develop swarms of autonomous, unwired RoboBees.

**"Bee" useful**
Many crops rely on bees to spread pollen among their flowers, so that fruits can grow. But some bees are disappearing at an alarming rate. Swarms of tiny robots like these RoboBees might one day have to take over pollinating duties.

# Robots that Slither and Crawl

The lowly snake has one of the most *versatile* (adaptable) forms in nature. Snakes have no arms, legs, fins, or wings. Yet they can slither, burrow, climb, swim, and even glide, all by simply changing their body shape. This versatility has inspired a number of snakelike robots, or snakebots.

Like living snakes, snakebots have long, slender, flexible bodies. This design offers several advantages. First, snakebots can slither

**This snakebot** created by researchers at Carnegie Mellon University in Pittsburgh helped rescue workers search for survivors after a 2017 earthquake in Mexico City.

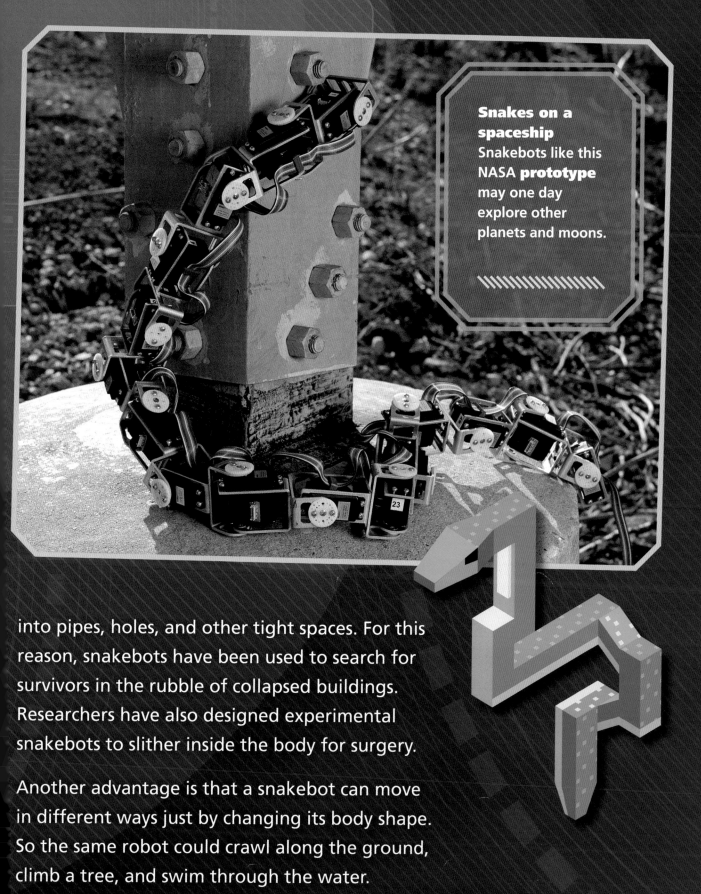

into pipes, holes, and other tight spaces. For this reason, snakebots have been used to search for survivors in the rubble of collapsed buildings. Researchers have also designed experimental snakebots to slither inside the body for surgery.

Another advantage is that a snakebot can move in different ways just by changing its body shape. So the same robot could crawl along the ground, climb a tree, and swim through the water.

[ 17 ]

A snakebot is often built as a "chain" of connected segments. Each segment may have its own motors, **sensors,** and **microprocessors.** This design makes it easy to change the snakebot's length by simply adding or removing segments. It also makes the snakebot resistant to damage. If one or more segments stop working, the rest may continue to function.

Snakes are not the only animals that can change the way they move. In 2013, Swiss inventors showed off an improved version of their robot Salamandra robotica. This 3-foot- (1-meter-) long robot is built to move like a salamander. The salamander is a four-legged amphibian that both can crawl on land and swim by whipping its snakelike body back and forth. Salamandra robotica mimics a living salamander, moving from land to water or water to land with ease.

**"Just call me Sal"**
Salamandra robotica is a salamanderlike robot that can switch from swimming to crawling with ease.

**Salamandra robotica** has helped researchers study how an animal's brain and nervous system controls its movements.

Crawling is not just for animals that live on the ground. Some small lizards called geckos can crawl up smooth surfaces and even hang upside down. Geckos climb using special *adhesive* (sticky) pads on their feet. The pads are covered with tiny hairs that only stick when pressed in a certain direction. Geckos can easily unstick their feet by pushing them the other way. Researchers at Stanford University in California have

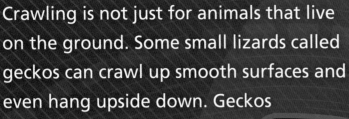

**Stickybot** can climb straight up glass surfaces with its gecko-inspired feet. Here the robot (center) is seen with its creators, Sangbae Kim (left) and Mark Cutkosky (right).

developed a robot named Stickybot that climbs much like a gecko. Stickybot can scale glass surfaces using pads of artificial adhesive on its feet.

Being able to move is one thing. Robots must also be able to navigate by sensing their surroundings. The robot SCRATCHbot navigates without the use of vision by mimicking a living scurrier—the rat. SCRATCHbot senses its surroundings using 18 robotic whiskers. The robot was designed by researchers at the University of Bristol in England in the early 2000's.

# Balancing Ballbot

Not all robots take their inspiration from nature. Some move in ways that are uniquely robotic. In 2005, inventors at Carnegie Mellon University introduced a new kind of robot called Ballbot. Ballbot is about the size of a human being. But it moves by balancing atop a single rolling ball.

Balancing in this way may seem like a circus act. But it actually solves some pesky problems that plague robots. Traditional robots have wide bases to avoid tipping over. But this shape makes it difficult for them to move in tight spaces. Traditional robots also tend to speed up and slow down very gradually, also to avoid tipping.

Ballbot can speed up and slow down relatively quickly, move in any direction, and turn on the spot. The robot uses motorized wheels to spin the ball in different directions, somewhat like a lumberjack rolling a log. Ballbot's ease of movement comes at a cost, however. Even when standing still, the robot must make constant, tiny adjustments to keep itself upright.

## Balancing act

Ballbot can guide a person by the hand, pull a person up from a sitting to standing position, and even help carry heavy things, all while balancing on a rolling ball. Its inventors hope that future ballbots will help the elderly and people with disabilities.

# Thinking inside the Ball

Some robots take the rolling ball concept even further, putting the entire robot inside the ball. These robots work a little bit like a hamster running inside an exercise ball. The robot has motorized wheels that turn against the outer shell, causing the ball to roll. The robot itself is weighted to stay upright as the ball around it moves. The result is a highly maneuverable robot that may be completely sealed from the outside world.

One of the strangest ball robots was Adelbrecht, made by the Dutch artist Martin Spanjaard in the 1980's. Adelbrecht was a ball 1 ⅓ foot (40 centimeters) across. It could roll around, talk, sense when it was being petted, and more.

**Adelbrecht,** a robot constructed as an art project, liked being petted. Its **autonomy** and curious interactions with people paved the way for today's robotic pets.

**Sphero's round plastic shell** protects the palm-sized robot from the elements, allowing it to cruise the great outdoors while other robots have to play inside.

In 2011, the Sphero company began selling toy ball robots that could fit in the palm of your hand. The robots are covered in a waterproof plastic ball. They can roll, turn, bounce, light up, and more. Sphero's ball robots are controlled wirelessly using an **app** on a cell phone or tablet computer.

HELLO, MY NAME IS:

# BB-8

Perhaps the most famous ball robot is the droid BB-8, introduced in the science fiction film *Star Wars: The Force Awakens* (2015). BB-8 is a rolling, rollicking robot. It has a dome-shaped head that slides freely over its ball-shaped body. BB-8 may look like a free-wheeler, but most of its scenes were shot using puppets. When it came time to make a toy version of the robot, the film's producers worked with the manufacturer Sphero. Sphero modified its self-contained ball robot, adding a dome-shaped head held in place magnetically.

## AUTONOMY

### MOVIE

HIGH

The movie droid BB-8 was about as close to a living companion as a Jedi could hope for.

### TOY

LOW

Toy BB-8's autonomy is a little more limited, but he can patrol your bedroom, respond to voice commands, and frighten the cat.

## SPECIAL ABILITIES

MOVIE: Movie BB-8 can co-pilot an X-wing starfighter.

TOY: Toy BB-8 can be controlled using a special Force Band worn on the wrist.

## MAKER

MOVIE: ???

TOY: The American company Sphero created toy BB-8.

## HEIGHT

MOVIE: 2 feet 2 inches (0.67 meters), slightly shorter than an Ewok

TOY: 4 ½ inches (11 centimeters), not quite as big as a grapefruit

# Robot Shapeshifters

Some robots are not limited to a single shape. In the late 1990's, inventors began experimenting with robots made up of building blocks called *modules.* The modules could be connected and reconnected in various arrangements. Such robots were said to be *modular.*

The first such robots were made up of modules that looked like hinges. Each module could bend and had its own motor and control system. When the modules were connected, each one could network with its neighbors. Together, the modules worked out how best to move the robot.

Later modular robots could be reconfigured. Imagine a robot made up of five or six modules. Connect the modules in a long chain, and the robot might slither, moving like a snake. Arrange them in an "H" shape, and the robot might crawl on four legs. Connect the modules in a loop, and the robot might roll along like a tire.

The first modular reconfigurable robots had to be taken apart and put together by hand. But in the early 2000's scientists began developing modules that could rearrange themselves.

**These 'bots are stacked!** Cubelets toys allow kids to build robots by connecting stackable cubes. The behavior of the robot depends on how the cubes are arranged.

# Smaller and Smaller

When it comes to robots, bigger is not always better. In fact, inventors have been working to make smaller and smaller robots for a variety of uses.

One such robot is Alice, developed in the late 1990's and early 2000's by inventors at the Swiss Federal Institute of Technology, in Lausanne. Alice is a cube-shaped robot measuring less than 1 inch (2.5 centimeters) on a side—little bigger than a sugar cube. Alice packs two

**Sweet robot**
The robot Alice is little bigger than a tricked-out sugar cube.

motors with wheels, proximity (nearness) **sensors,** a rechargeable battery, and more into that tiny frame.

Even Alice looks huge compared with a ladybug-sized robot introduced in 2009 as part of a European project called I-SWARM. That robot measures about $\frac{1}{10}$ inch (3 millimeters) in length. It has a solar cell for power and visual sensors. But the robot is too small to include traditional motors. Rather, it scoots along using a **piezoelectric actuator**—a piece of material that changes shape in response to an electric charge.

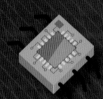

# Robot Swarms

Tiny robots may not seem all that useful on their own. But many are designed to cooperate in large groups called swarms. **Robot swarms** take their inspiration from social insects, such as ants and bees. Individual insects have pretty simple brains. But working together, social insects can do some amazing things.

Many ants, for example, seem to move in fairly random patterns. They simply avoid obstacles

**A single ant can't do much.** But working together in a swarm, a colony of ants can build huge nests, manage insect "livestock," and farm fungus for food.

in their path. They also lay and follow trails of chemicals called pheromones. Through a combination of these two simple behaviors, ants can develop surprisingly efficient paths from their nest to food sources.

In 2013, researchers showed that a swarm of Alice robots could navigate a maze in a similar manner. The robots were able to determine the most efficient route through the maze by leaving and following a trail of light, rather than pheromones.

**Maze runners**
Tiny Alice robots can navigate a maze by working together, in much the same way ants do. This ability may help future robot swarms work together to do amazing things.

In the 2010's, inventors at Harvard University demonstrated a swarm of tiny robots called Kilobots. *Kilo* means *one-thousand,* and the Harvard swarm features over a thousand robots—1,024, to be exact. Each kilobot is slightly smaller than a golf ball, standing a little over 1 inch (3 centimeters) tall. The inventors designed the robots to be cheap, so that they could be used in large numbers. Motorized wheels, for example, can be costly. So a Kilobot skitters along on a tripod of legs. The inventors showed that Kilobots could work together to arrange themselves in various formations, including letters and other shapes.

Inventors hope to develop robot swarms that can search for survivors following a disaster. **Swarm robots** may also be useful in space exploration. Imagine replacing a single, large space probe with a swarm of tiny ones. If some of the probes stop working, the rest could still continue the mission. The United States military has experimented to determine if swarm robots could conduct coordinated attacks on the battlefield.

**Kilobots won't kill your budget**
One of the Kilobots' main advantages is that they are cheap. Each **prototype** costs about $14 in parts.

# Nanobots

If smaller can be better, why not keep shrinking? Since the 1950's, inventors and science fiction authors have been fascinated with the idea of tiny robots called **nanobots.** Nanobots are designed to work on scales of 1 to 100 nanometers. A nanometer equals one-billionth of a meter (0.000000001 meter or $1/25,400,000$ inch). This is about $1/100,000$ the width of a human hair or 3 to 5 times the diameter of a single atom.

**Microscopic machinery**
Scientists are racing to create ever-smaller machinery, such as these tiny gears and chain. Each link on the chain is thinner than a human hair.

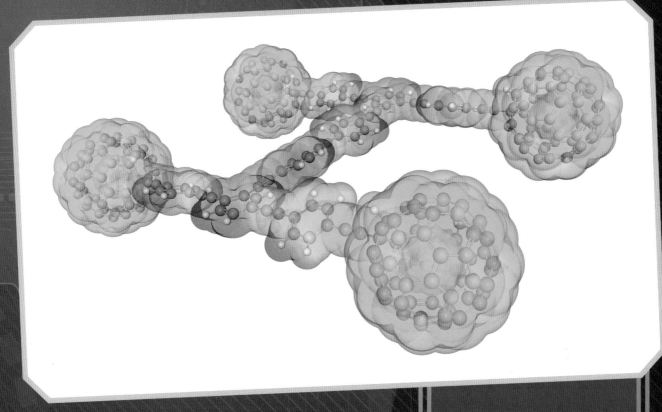

Swarms of nanobots might be able to do all kinds of amazing things. They could custom-build items one atom at a time. They could also operate inside the human body, destroying germs and repairing tissue.

Working mechanical nanobots are probably decades in the future. But inventors have already demonstrated some nanobotlike technology. In 2017, for example, inventors at Rice University in Houston, Texas, demonstrated a two-wheeled nanocar made out of a single molecule (group of atoms). The microscopic vehicle was a mere 1.5 nanometers across.

**Diminutive drag racers**
Scientists have created several tiny "nanocars" that can race across special tracks. The small dots in this illustration are individual atoms.

# Gray Goo

It would take huge swarms of **nanobots** to do most jobs. What is the best way to make all those nanobots? One solution would be to develop nanobots that self-replicate—that is, assemble more of their own kind from materials in their environment.

Self-replication can be a dangerous thing, however. The nanotechnology pioneer K. Eric Drexler described a self-replicating nanomachine in his book *Engines of Creation* (1986). Drexler imagined a tiny device that made a copy of itself every 1,000 seconds. So after 1,000 seconds, there would be two devices. In the next 1,000 seconds, those two devices would make two more, for a total of four, and so on.

Nanobots are small, but this kind of multiplication adds up quickly. In less than a day, there would be more than 1 ton (0.9 metric tons) of nanodevices. In less than two days, the devices would outweigh Earth. This idea stoked fears that out-of-control replicators might quickly use up all the available matter on Earth's surface, reducing it to a "gray goo" made up of nanobots. Drexler and many other scientists, however, think people overestimate the danger of a gray goo scenario.

## Big gooey mess?

Some people fear that self-replicating nanobots could multiply out of control, turning all the matter on Earth's surface into a "gray goo" of nanobots. It is a popular theme in science fiction, as shown in these images from film and television.

# Soft Robots

Most robots are hardbodies. Their surfaces are covered in hard metal or rigid plastic. But since the early 2000's, some inventors have been working to make a softer, gentler kind of robot. Soft robots are made of a flexible material such as rubber or plastic. These materials can move and bend when air or another fluid is pushed through them.

Soft robots have some advantages over traditional hard robots. First, a hard robot can only move at a limited number of joints. But a soft robot can change its entire body shape. Soft robots can also be more gentle, making it easier for them to work around people or handle delicate objects.

Inventors have experimented with soft robotic "fish" that swim much like the real thing. Manufacturers make soft robot **grippers** for handling fruit and other delicate, oddly shaped products.

**Mmm...donuts...**
Soft robotic grippers can pick up delicate items, such as food, that traditional robot grippers might mangle.

**"How do you do, fellow fish?"**
This soft robot created by researchers at the Massachusetts Institute of Technology (MIT) can swim with the fishes. But these fish don't look like they're buying it.

HELLO, MY NAME IS:

# Octobot

Even the
softest robots
tend to have some hard
parts, such as batteries
and computer chips. But not the robotic octopus
nicknamed Octobot. In 2016, Octobot became
the first **autonomous** robot made entirely from
soft parts. Unlike other soft robots, Octobot
does not rely on batteries, motors, and pumps to
move fluids through its body. Instead, chemical
reactions inside Octobot turn hydrogen peroxide
fuel into a gas. The gas inflates Octobot's
tentacles, causing them to move.

## AUTONOMY

**LOW**

Octobot cannot do much yet, but it does not need outside control or power systems to do it.

## SOFTNESS

Octobot's body contains no rigid parts.

## FLUID CONTROL

Most robots are controlled by electric charges zipping through rigid computer chips. Octobot is controlled by fluids moving through a device called a microfluidic logic circuit.

## PRINT ON DEMAND

Much of Octobot's body is made using 3-D printing techniques.

## MAKER

Octobot was developed by researchers at Harvard University.

# Inspired by Origami

Some robots are so flexible, they can do something other robots cannot—they can fold. Researchers have developed several robots with folding parts inspired by origami, the traditional Japanese art of folding paper.

## A 'bot-ter pill to swallow

This tiny origami robot could someday unfold itself from a swallowed capsule and crawl across the stomach to remove a swallowed object or patch a wound.

In 2015, inventors at the Massachusetts Institute of Technology (MIT) demonstrated a tiny robot assembled from a flat sheet of plastic. The plastic folds itself into a robot in the presence of heat. The robot can scurry, carry loads, and push obstacles out of its way. It can even dissolve into a liquid when no longer needed. In 2017, the researchers showed that the same robot could take on and use a number of folding exoskeletons (outer coverings). The exoskeletons transform the robot from a walker to a roller or even a boat.

Also in 2017, researchers at Harvard University and MIT showed off robot "muscles" inspired by origami. The muscles have a folding core surrounded by a "skin" of plastic or fabric. Pumping water or air out of the muscle causes it to contract (get shorter). The muscle may also curl, bend, or grip, in various ways, depending on how the core is folded. The invention could be used in soft robotic muscles and grippers.

**Squishy but strong**
Soft robots are often weaklings, but these soft robot muscles demonstrated in 2017 are heavy lifters. They can hold up to 1,000 times their weight.

# Glossary

**actuator**  a device, such as a motor, that provides movement to a robot.

**app**  a simple computer program, often designed to be run on a smartphone or tablet computer; short for application.

**autonomy**  the degree to which a robot can make decisions without input from a human operator to achieve a goal.

**drone**  an uncrewed aerial vehicle. Most drones are piloted remotely, but some are autonomous.

**gripper**  a device used for grabbing something; a robot "hand."

**hexapod**  a robot with six legs.

**humanoid**  shaped like or resembling a human.

**microprocessor**  the device that does the actual computing in a computer.

**nanobots**  very small robots designed to work on scales of 1 to 100 nanometers. A nanometer equals one-billionth of a meter (0.000000001 meter or $1/25,400,000$ inch).

**piezoelectric actuator**  an actuator powered by a piece of piezoelectric material, which changes shape in response to an electric current.

**prototype**  an original model on which a design is based.

**sensor**  a device that takes in information from the outside world and translates it into code.

**swarm robots**  small robots designed to work in large groups.

# Additional Resources

De La Rosa, Jeff. *Meet NASA Inventor Mason Peck and His Team's Squishy, Fishy Robot Explorers.* Chicago: World Book, Inc., 2017.

Faust, Daniel. *Underwater Robots.* New York: PowerKids, 2017.

Graham, Ian. *You Wouldn't Want to Live Without Robots!* New York: Franklin Watts, 2019.

Smibert, Angie. *Building Better Robots.* North Mankato, MN: 12-Story Library, 2017.


**Boston Dynamics**
https://www.bostondynamics.com/

**Bristol Robotics Laboratory**
http://www.brl.ac.uk/default.aspx

**EPFL - Biorobotics Laboratory**
https://biorob.epfl.ch/page-36354.html

**IEEE - Robots**
https://robots.ieee.org/

# Acknowledgments

| | |
|---|---|
| Cover: | © Ociacia/Shutterstock |
| 4-5 | NASA; © Lori Sanders, Harvard University; Mark R. Cutkosky, Stanford University; Sangbae Kim, MIT |
| 6-7 | NASA/JPL-Caltech |
| 8-9 | © Festo |
| 10-11 | FZI Research Center for Information Technology (licensed under CC BY-SA 3.0) |
| 12-13 | © Bruce Frisch, Science Source |
| 14-15 | © AeroVironment; © Kevin Ma and Pakpong Chirarattananon, Harvard University |
| 16-17 | NASA |
| 18-19 | Kostas Karakasiliotis, Biorobotics Laboratory/EPFL |
| 20-21 | Mark R. Cutkosky, Stanford University; Sangbae Kim, MIT; © Mr.B-king/Shutterstock |
| 22-23 | © Carnegie Mellon University; Unagaraj (licensed under CC BY-SA 3.0) |
| 24-25 | © V2_ Lab for the Unstable Media; © Sphero |
| 26-27 | © Lucasfilm Ltd./Sphero |
| 28-29 | © Modular Robotics |
| 30-31 | © Swiss Federal Institute of Technology in Zurich; © Erik Edqvist, Uppsala University |
| 32-33 | © Alfonso de Tomas, Shutterstock; © Simon Garnier, Swarm Lab |
| 34-35 | Asus Creative (licensed under CC BY-SA 4.0) |
| 36-37 | Sandia National Laboratories; Edumol Molecular Visualizations (licensed under CC BY-SA 2.0) |
| 38-39 | © Twentieth Century Fox |
| 40-41 | © Soft Robotics, Inc.; © Joseph DelPreto, MIT CSAIL |
| 42-43 | © Lori Sanders, Harvard University |
| 44-45 | © Melanie Gonick, MIT; © Shuguang Li, Wyss Institute at Harvard University |

# Index